Terrorism and Kids:
Comforting Your Child

by Fern Reiss

10% of the proceeds of this book will be donated to the American Red Cross Disaster Relief Fund

Peanut Butter and Jelly Press
Boston, Massachusetts

This book is dedicated to the memory of those who died on September 11, 2001:
Brave firemen, pilots and flight attendants, helpless passengers, World Trade Center victims, and all the unknowing men, women, and children who were in the wrong place at the wrong time.

We grieve for you, and mourn with your families.
Our nation—and our world—will never be the same.

For information on quantity discounts to schools and groups, or premium sales to corporations, please contact the publisher:

Peanut Butter and Jelly Press
P.O. Box 590239
Newton, MA 02459-0002
(617) 630-0945
info@PeanutButterandJellyPress.com
www.PeanutButterandJellyPress.com

Library of Congress Cataloging-in-Publication Data

Reiss, Fern.
    Terrorism and kids : comforting your child / by Fern Reiss.
        p. cm.
    ISBN 1-893290-09-3 (pbk.)
    1. Children and terrorism. 2. Child rearing. I. Title.
    HQ784.T45 R44 2001
    649'.1—dc21   2001006671

10 9 8 7 6 5 4 3 2

Acknowledgements

I would like to thank the people who helped me work through the weighty and difficult issues in this book, so that it would be accessible to parents and teachers and address the very real problems we face in processing these situations with our children.

Thanks to all the psychologists, the doctors, and the stress counselors who shared their thoughts with me. Thanks especially to psychotherapist Aviva Bock and psychiatrist Dr. Mindy Shankman. Without your psychological nudges I never could have done it.

Thanks to everyone who helped me rush this book into production in two days, nine months earlier than scheduled. I would especially like to thank my cover designer, Mayapriya Long of BookWrights, and Pat Holt of Holt Uncensored.

Thanks to my many communities, including Shaarei; the homeschoolers; the Your Money or Your Lifers, and finally the members of pub-forum, who have contributed so much to my growth in and knowledge of the publishing world.

Thanks to our many Israeli friends and relatives who live under the constant shadow of terrorism, and especially to Sue and Avie, Mira, Susan and Yedidya, and Moira and Danny. This book was originally written with you in mind.

Thanks to my children, Benjamin, Daniel Yedidya, and Ariel. You helped me to understand what the questions were, and forced me to find good answers. This was never a research project or dispassionate assignment; it was something I needed to do to work it through for my own wonderful kids. You guys are the best.

Finally, thank you to Jonathan, who fed, clothed, bathed (well, once, anyway), and cared for everyone, including our nursing infant, in the aftermath of the tragedy and an intense week of writing. I never could have done it without you and a more wonderful husband does not exist.

Contents

Preface

Years ago, when I was a sophomore in college, I spent a year living in Israel. Except for college and summer camp, both pretty sheltered environments, it was my first real experience away from home.

It was a wonderful year in almost every way: Fun activities, fantastic people, educational and challenging experiences. But there was one experience that stands out in my mind, that I think about still.

I was in the center of Jerusalem, sitting in a crowded café and sipping iced coffee, which in Israel comes with a tremendous scoop of chocolate ice cream. As I gleefully licked off the spoon I heard someone close by scream "Hafetz Hashud, Suspicious Object!" Immediately, the happy buzz in the café ceased; people jumped up and ran in all directions, soldiers appeared right and left, and one small child—who a minute earlier had been eyeing my ice cream hungrily—began screaming.

It was a false alarm, and after the object was poked and prodded by the soldiers, it was declared to be just an ordinary, empty paper bag. But I'll never forget the anxiety, the sense of my heart beating overly fast, the way time seemed to simultaneously speed up and slow down. I'll never forget the look of horror, and then the heartbreaking relief, in that small child's eyes.

We Americans have been lucky, for the most part: Terrorism lives in the world around us, but rarely knocks at our door. When it does—as it did that awful September 11, as it may never do again—we need to be united as a nation. In addition to seeking justice, we need to work through our fear, and our anger, and our grieving.

But most of all, we need to protect our children, who don't have an innate ability to deal with these events. We need to shield them while simultaneously allowing them to actively work through trauma that no one would wish on them. We need to listen to them, and encourage them to talk. We need to comfort them, cuddle them, and hear their fears very carefully. That is what this book is about.

Introduction

Terrorism and kids are two words that should not appear in the same sentence. As awful a specter as terrorism is, it is that much worse coupled with children. Children, regardless of the situation, irrespective of the circumstances, can be nothing but helpless bystanders.

Yet throughout the world there are countries whose children habitually see the face of terrorism, some on a regular, even daily basis. Until recently, the United States was relatively immune.

What happened on September 11, 2001 will live in infamy forever. The newscasts and reports of that day and its aftermath are printed indelibly on our minds. How long will it take to erase the images? Even those not directly affected by the death of a friend or a loved one have cried, have mourned, have grieved. There are no adults in the country who have escaped unscathed.

What about the children?

Yet how much worse it is for our children! As adults, we can hear the news and be fearful. But for our children, incomplete understanding coupled with an awareness of our fear is simply terrifying.

For most children, hijacking is something that happens in the movies. Plane crashes are events that occur in cartoons. Smallpox is an illness from the "old days." And death is not real. Until now.

Not only have American children never experienced terrorism: They have never experienced Depression, war, or national trauma of any sort. Although individual children have certainly survived abuse of various kinds, as a nation, American kids have had the carefree childhood that we barely appreciated in the moment, and can only now look back upon nostalgically and sadly.

And in some ways, the hardest part is watching the rest of us unravel. Accustomed to a routine, to a world that is fairly invariable, children are disturbed by seeing their parents weeping for reasons they don't fully understand, seeing flags at half mast without appreciating the import, watching America grieve and fear something they can not–and should not have to—understand.

In America, the closest experience we have to dealing with terrorism is dealing with trauma. Childhood trauma can be caused by a number of things including abuse, kidnappings, and accidents. But until recently, never terrorism.

Who is this book for?

This book was written to give parents and teachers some guidance in dealing with children and answering their difficult questions following a terrorist attack. There are no perfect answers or solutions to tragedy, but this book offers ideas.

It is meant for the nation's many children who were not directly involved in the terrorist attack, but who heard about it and are struggling with its implications and the palpable aura of fear it has created.

If your child was actually on the scene, or if you have a close family member who was killed in a recent terrorist activity, please also seek professional counseling. This book, and those listed in the bibliography, may be helpful, but can not replace the interaction with a trained professional grief and trauma therapist.

Remember that even children not physically present at an event may experience trauma. Studies have shown that even those not physically present at the site of a trauma were later shown to have experienced emotional harm; for example, psychiatrists who studied the aftermath of a dam collapse in West Virginia discovered that even those adults not physically in the valley at the time of the flood suffered emotional trauma.

Thus, children who view a terrorist incident on television, for example, may be adversely affected. In addition, traumatic effects may be "contagious" in the sense that they may spread from actual victims to others who were never victims at all.

How is terrorism different?

One of the key differences is that terrorism is a group event in a way that kidnappings, abuse, fires, accidents, and hospital operations are not. In some types of trauma, such as abuse, children are singled out for malevolent attention; in others, the trauma is the result of an accident, be it a fire or a car crash. In both situations, the child, or perhaps the child and his immediate family, is the sole object of such attention. The rest of the child's world—his family, his school, or his larger community—are oblivious of, or indifferent to, the trauma that is unfolding.

Of course, this in no way minimizes the effects of such trauma on the individual child and family. Nonetheless, the larger world around them continues to exist unscathed. Although earth-shattering to the child and family involved, such trauma is not a group event.

...ent, by contrast, is not specifically directed
...child himself. One might think the child would
...feel less singled out, less vulnerable, less personally
...ed. Strangely, this is not the case: Merely viewing the
...vents on television can be traumatic. In fact, studies show
that mere witnesses are actually *more* likely to turn violent in
the future than the primary victims of the terrorist attack.

In a terrorist attack, it is not only the child undergoing the
trauma: All his communal supports are stressed. His entire
lifestyle is under attack. It is his parents, usually the stars he
navigates by, who have gone awry and broken down in tears
or anger. It is the adults around him who suddenly act
strangely. It is his whole neighborhood, city, and country
which are suddenly in disarray. It is his routine, the very
fabric of his existence, that is uprooted and ignored as
everyone is glued to a television set and immersed in grief
and anger instead of performing normal roles and rituals.

Because a terrorist incident is a group event, there is a
second impact. Since the family, school, neighborhood, and
country are facing the same circumstance, everyone's
attention—even that of the children's parents—is diverted

18

from their traumatized children. Parents and teachers experience their own difficulties in dealing with the situation.

Contrast that with other traumatic situations: When your child undergoes a hospital operation, you know you need to be there for him. But when the whole country is reeling under the impact of a terrorist attack, it's difficult to remember that your child is experiencing the same situation even more acutely.

Parents find it difficult to be there for their children when they themselves are in the midst of the same traumatic circumstances. It's difficult to feel confident, powerful, and in-charge when faced with such terrible events. When you as a parent are immobilized by feelings of helplessness, it is difficult to muster the strength you need to console your child.

Parents are also unprepared for the changes such an incident inflicts on their child. A child who has gone through what we might term *usual* trauma—an operation, a fire, or a car accident, for example—might be cosseted and babied by her parents for weeks or months, in clear acknowledgement that trauma has occurred.

A child who has merely heard radio reports of terrorism, on the other hand, is often ignored as a serious victim. It is only after their children turn into different children, exhibiting unusual and generally undesirable behavior, that some parents think to question whether it might be trauma.

For your children, this is a horrifying event that they have experienced, and the fact that they have only witnessed it on television or heard about it on the radio in no way lessens the gravity of their loss of security. According to trauma experts, children's feelings of helplessness during a terrorist attack may cause them to fear loss of family and loss of their own lives, as well as a presentiment that worse things will follow. Although the event itself may resolve, the child's terror lingers.

One final way in which terrorism is different from most other traumatic situations for children is in the perception of widespread violence and malevolence. When a child is in a car crash, for example, it is probably only that situation—

traumatic though it may be—which is frightening. Although a child who is a victim of a car crash may refuse to ride in cars, they probably won't see the whole world through dark glasses.

Contrast that with the child who has experienced the fallout of a terrorist attack: In a terrorism situation, it seems that the entire world is full of bad guys, that there are whole groups of evil people running around freely. It is suddenly not the particulars of a given situation, but the whole world that has become dark, gloomy, and full of nasty surprises. The world is no longer a safe place. Terrorism can alter forever your child's feelings about her life and her world.

Will my child be ok?

It is undeniable that many American children have been, and will continue to be, affected by terrorism. This book gives parents and teachers techniques to minimize terrorism's impact.

Ultimately, however, most children are resilient. By all means use the techniques in this book to help your child through these difficult days—but don't spend too much time worrying.

Don't assume that your child's lack of interest is necessarily denial. For many children, terrorism is mere background noise, completely irrelevant to their lives. Even if your children seem obsessed with the recent events, don't assume they're traumatized. Kids are emotionally stronger than they look. Your child will probably be fine.

What's inside

The chapter *Strategies for Helping Your Child* discusses concrete strategies for helping your child in the aftermath of a terrorist attack. It discusses how to handle television and radio reports, how to tailor your emotional response, how to offer reassurance, and how to talk to your children. It gives specific suggestions for minimizing the impact of a terrorist activity—keeping to routines, maintaining behavior standards, and the like. It surveys symptoms to watch for in your children such as recklessness, personality changes, and complaints about physical symptoms. It also reminds parents that they need to comfort themselves in this trying time.

The chapter *Tailoring Your Approach to the Age of Your Child* describes how to talk to your children, based on their age and developmental level. It discusses how infants, preschoolers, grade schoolers and teenagers understand events differently, and how you should tailor your words and actions to each of these age groups.

The chapter *Answering Children's Questions* elaborates on the different questions children will ask in these circumstances. It includes general questions such as "Will it happen here?" and specific questions, such as "What about anthrax and smallpox?" You'll learn strategies for dealing with your child's reluctance to return to school, his hesitancy to laugh and smile, her worries about dwelling on horrific thoughts, and his fears of never returning to normalcy again.

The chapter *Writing, Drawing, and Playing as Therapy* explores using writing, drawing, and playing as aids to help your child work through the trauma. It gives concrete suggestions of how to encourage your child to explore his feelings by inviting him to draw, write and play. Studies have shown that children who are able to express their fears and inner terrors in these ways bounce back faster.

Finally, the bibliography shares other resources that may be helpful in dealing with a terrorist situation, including books for parents and children on grief, death, and trauma.

Strategies for Helping Your Child

There are no easy answers for how to make everything better after a terrorist attack has shaken your world, particularly since much of the horror is ongoing. But there are many things you can do and say to help lessen the impact for your children. In employing the specific strategies below, there are a few things to keep in mind.

First, both adults and children are likely to experience some amount of shock and denial after a terrorist attack or other severe trauma. According to the American Psychological Association, these are normal, protective reactions and are likely to be experienced by almost everyone. Your emotional state may be extremely fragile temporarily, leaving you feeling stunned. You and your child may feel unable to internalize that the terrorist attack has occurred.

You may also distance yourself from experiencing the full intensity of the attack. You and your child may temporarily feel numb and disconnected from life.

In the days and weeks that follow, you and your child may experience unusually intense emotions, greater irritability, nervous tension, depression, or dramatic mood swings. You may engage in more family fights and conflicts. You or your child may have recurring vivid flashbacks of the attack accompanied by sweating, rapid heart beat, nausea, and chest pain. Normal concentration, sleep, and eating patterns may also be affected.

Be aware that all of these are normal reactions to severe stress, and that with time, the symptoms will lessen. In addition, here are several strategies for helping your child deal with the incident.

Limit television and internet viewing

In the initial aftermath of a terrorist attack, try to limit your child's visual exposure to the situation. Pictures are far more disturbing to children than words.

By limiting television viewing during these situations, and confining yourself to radio and print media, you will go a long way towards limiting the scary pictures that your child will later recall.

Television or internet images of terrorism, under the best of circumstances, can be violent and repetitive. Under the worst of circumstances, these media may show situations to which you would never willingly subject your child. The trauma of the imagery is certainly more powerful than the same words spoken in a radio report or read aloud from a newspaper.

"We heard all the reports on the radio, and because of that, I think, our children seem much less bothered than most of our friends kids," one parent noted. "It's not quite as real to them, and they seem to be forgetting it faster."

Don't make the mistake of thinking that little children, who may buzz in and out of a room or seem not to be paying attention, are not affected. Their radar is exceptionally tuned for such things, and especially since you will exhibit some emotions while watching, they are sure to be paying attention.

Finally, studies have shown that children who watch a lot of television violence of any sort—whether the news of terrorist attacks or just fictional movies—feel less physically safe than children who watch less violence.

Turn the television off.

Limit your news viewing

Too much watching or listening to terrorism situations can lead to feelings of helplessness, lethargy, and despair. In fact, studies show that the news coverage isn't always even an accurate portrayal of a situation: For example, though statistics report a decrease in the incidence of crime, reporting of crime in the news has increased. The more news your child is exposed to, the more helpless and powerless he is likely to feel.

Studies have also shown that traumatic events that occur over an extended period of time may cause greater distress in children than relatively brief events. The longer you leave the news on, the longer your child perceives the length of the terrorist attack.

"It seemed to be going on forever, this endless disaster" one mother said afterwards. "We spent all of September 11th glued to the television set. It felt like a week."

So try to curtail your news time. Despite the fact that it's somehow mesmerizing to fixate on the radio and listen obsessively as they describe the unfolding scenario over and over, it is no healthier for you than it is for your kids. Listen to the news, but set limits on your listening: Try tuning in once an hour for updates, rather than leaving the radio on non-stop.

If you have young children, consider listening with headphones. Better yet, if the weather's pleasant bring the radio outside and listen discreetly while they zoom around on bikes or in trees. Children are better able to process horrifying news when they hear about it without the immediacy of television or radio.

In between situations, leave the radio off completely. Make sure you have plenty of "normal" days so that your child's whole world doesn't become news immersion—with all the fear that brings.

Don't let your children listen alone

Don't leave your youngsters listening to the news reports alone. Stay in the room: Your physical presence is calming in such scary times. Staying available to them also means that you can model behavior for them.

Young children, in particular, may not have the verbal capacity to express their feelings, but by keeping them with you while you process the evolving information you can allow them to express themselves physically in your presence.

"My three-year-old's response was to race around the room like a maniac, and I know that was his way of processing the whole thing," said a mother of two boys. "He could have done it in the other room or outside, but his running around me was his way of shaking off the experience, I think, under my gaze."

Grief therapists, using the work of John Bowlby, name four stages everyone experiences after a bereavement: denial, anger, despair, and acceptance. In a terrorism situation, we might add one more: Fear.

Cuddle your children as you hear the news. The physical contact, and the familiar feel of your embrace, will do a great deal to comfort your child.

Slightly older children will be able to obtain access to the news themselves unless you take precautions. Have a frank conversation with your child and explain why you'd like them not to listen to the radio or watch television without you. If you are afraid your child might forget or not listen, consider removing radios, computers, and televisions (or television antennas) from the premises for the duration.

And remember that elementary school children can read. Be careful about leaving the newspaper around the house.

Exhibit your emotions

Keeping a tight rein on your emotions may be one of the worst things you can do. Children need to see you react. These situations are scary. Respond to that. Sigh. Rant. Cry.

These are normal reactions to extreme stress—and your child needs to see that they are permissible reactions. Otherwise, your child's emotions will stay bottled up inside her—which isn't healthy.

Earl Grollman, national expert on counseling children about death, says that if you repress your feelings, your child is more likely to keep her own emotions at bay. And children are particularly sensitive during a crisis, according to a report by the American Academy of Child and Adolescent Psychiatry. Children receive implicit permission to mourn from adults if they see their adults mourning. Give them that permission.

On the other hand, make sure that your child realizes that although you're sad and angry, you're not angry at *him*. Children often feel responsible for events, but by cuddling them while listening, you can reassure them that your emotions are not directed at them.

"My kids seemed quite relieved to see that my anger had nothing to do with them. I guess often when I'm yelling I'm yelling at them," said a father right after a terrorist incident. "This time, they knew it had nothing to do with them, because we were all sat on the couch together."

You'll also find it healthier for you to allow your emotions to flow naturally, rather than keeping a tight rein on them.

Offer personal reassurance

Even while you are watching the television describe horrifying events, stress to your child that although awful, they are happening to other people, far away. Be emphatic that their immediate support systems—your family, your friends, your neighbors—are safe and sound.

This is important even if you live quite far from the tragedy. Children are comforted by hearing that their relatives and friends are safe, especially when confronted with such devastation.

Also, point out that even though one area had an earthquake, most areas are fine; Even though a plane was hijacked, almost all plane rides are uneventful. The point to convey is that bad things only happen once in a very long while.

Make sure that your child knows where the events occurred, if far away. Most young children don't have a clear sense of physical distance. It may be very helpful to your child to understand how far away your town is from New York. Expressing the distance in time ("It would take me twenty days to get there if we started walking now") rather than mileage which they don't understand, is helpful for young children.

"Oh, that's where we went on vacation last year," said one four year old of an incident in New York. "That's very far away."

On the other hand, don't expect that your reassurances will magically solve your child's problems. Just because you tell them that they're safe, your children's fears may not evaporate. Cynthia Monahon, in her book "Children and Trauma: A Guide for Parents and Professionals" calls children's memories of trauma "tyrannical" and points out that healing takes time.

Keep to your routine

Keep the children's routine as close to usual as possible. Obviously if everyone in the house is home listening to the radio then your child can't be at his violin lesson. But varying children's routines—even for happy occasions like vacations—can be disorienting for them. Everyone knows that infants and toddlers do best with a "regular" naptime and bedtime; routines of some sort are equally important to older children. In terrorism situations this is even more true.

"Our kids were pretty upset while seeing the news, but then we did all our usual things—dinner as a family, story time, bath time. By bedtime they seemed completely comforted—as if the routines oriented them," noticed one mother.

Studies have shown that the child's perception of the outcome of the situation affects their distress level. Children whose lives are negatively altered after the initial events suffer greater distress than children who view the event as one isolated negative blip on the horizon. So try to keep to your regular routine, in the hope that this normalcy will keep the situation contained.

Try to remember to make time for meals, and have them in the same place as usual; read the same goodnight stories, and conduct the bedtime ritual you always do. These routines will help your child orient himself and calm his feelings of the world being out of whack. Routines are a familiar haven in a sea of strangeness.

And don't forget to make some time for family fun, despite the events of the world. Children need fun in their lives, regardless of the world situation.

Talk to your children

Children need to hear you process the situation—so they know what to make of it. By talking to your child as an incident is occurring, you bring them into the experience with you, rather than leaving them puzzled and alone on the periphery. Let them know that you are stunned, saddened, horrified.

But don't overdo your explanations, either.

"I was thinking I should explain the whole thing to them—you know, the politics of the countries involved, a sort of a logical justification of how those terrorists must have been thinking," said the father of three. "And then I thought, aw, heck with it. How do you explain something completely inexplicable, something beyond understanding, anyway?"

Admit to your child that these are difficult issues, and that sometimes it's hard to know how to think about things like this. Some problems don't have easy answers, and children do better if their adults admit that, rather than trying to give pat answers that don't satisfy.

If you have opinions on the politics of the situation, or ideas on how the government should respond, share those thoughts with your children. Such conversations will help them feel included—and empowered.

Talk at your child's level

Consider the age of your child. For example, infants pick up on the anxieties and actions of those around them and may be fussier than is usual. Try to be calm when interacting with your infant, and keep their routine the same.

For toddlers, keeping their routines is paramount. If they ask questions, make sure you answer simply and tell them that you'll keep them safe.

"My two year old just wanted to be held and comforted all day," said one mom.

Preschoolers don't understand a lot of what is happening. For example, most preschoolers do not understand that death is permanent; they think of it as a vacation that someone comes back from. Make sure you spend the time to deal with their questions and misperceptions.

Preschoolers, in particular, may have a difficult time because of their inability to separate reality from fantasy. According to Joanne Cantor, author of "Mommy, I'm Scared-How TV and Movies Frighten Children and What We Can Do To Protect Them," preschoolers are as terrified when Pinocchio turns into a donkey as they are by a story on a school shooting. Particularly after experiencing the heightened emotions of everyone around them after a terrorist incident, your preschooler may think that *everything* on television is real.

School age children are more interested in the events that are happening, but are less capable than older children of communicating. Reassure them that your family will be safe.

Contrary to what you might assume, teenagers particularly need the presence of an adult, because they will understand the situation enough to be terrified. Share your feelings with them honestly, and encourage them to share theirs.

And let them talk to you

Sometimes the best way for children to process such a situation is to talk about it. Let them. Do not force them to talk if they are not ready. But try not to shut down such conversations, if they start, even though you may feel uneasy and not know quite what to say. Ask open-ended, rather than yes/no questions, to try to elicit things that might otherwise stay buried.

"I thought my kids were ok with it, because I asked them and they said they were fine," one mother confided. "Then I read something that suggested asking what color they felt the world was this week. And two of them said black! And then the whole thing came pouring out—a lot more grief and anxiety than I would ever have known about otherwise."

Ask what your child already knows. This way you can clarify distortions, and help the child get accurate information. How many 4-year-olds really understand what it means to be hijacked? But don't be too quick to jump in with advice and information. Wait to find out what your child is feeling before offering an opinion.

Also, make sure that each child has some alone time with you. If they seek you out while you're doing the dishes or at your computer, make the time for them that moment: Later they might be unable to verbalize what they wanted to share. Be alert for times when they are more likely to talk.

Try to concentrate your talking time in the earlier parts of the day. Discussing terrorism right before bedtime is a surefire way to encourage nightmares. Instead, use the time before bed to read a comforting book, play a board game, or simply spend some time cuddling. Talk in the morning; snuggle at night.

And let them say what they want

Children can have strong feelings, sometimes exceedingly unpleasant feelings. If, in the weeks after a terrorist incident, you allow your child to express himself as he likes, without censure or judgment, it will prevent his feelings from being expressed in more disturbing behaviors, and he will heal faster.

Your child may also have violent revenge fantasies that he elaborates in gory detail. As long as he is not acting on these fantasies, accept them as part of his healing process, disturbing though they may be.

Or your child may have particularly sad and gloomy feelings, which may be difficult for you to hear.

One mother told me, "I thought my child was completely ok while we were talking about it. And then when I tucked him in he added, "And please God, protect us against terrorism," in his prayers. I was heartbroken."

Let your child verbalize the situation as he needs to, whatever expression that takes. If he wants to talk about it with you, encourage him, whether or not you like how he is talking.

If you're uncomfortable with how an older child is talking about the situation, it's ok to admit that. Saying something like, "I understand how strongly you feel about this, though it makes me sad to hear you talk about other people that way," is ok for your child to hear; chances are they'll see it in your face whether or not you verbalize it. But make sure your child understands that even though his thoughts may occasionally make you uncomfortable, you still want to hear them.

"I'm sorry the world is making you feel so sad right now, but I'm glad we can talk about it," one mother told her daughter.

Don't lie to your children

Don't be dishonest in answering your children's questions. If they ask if people died, admit the truth. But don't go into more details than they are interested in, either: Don't volunteer this information unless they ask you. Listen carefully to be sure you are only answering what they want to hear.

"Janie asked what happened, but it turned out she didn't really want to know all the details. She just wanted to know why the radio was on. We told her we were listening to some sad news, and that satisfied her," said one mother.

When children perceive the event—correctly or incorrectly—as life threatening to them, they feel more disruption than when they perceive it as a removed threat. Thus, without lying about the details, attempt to in some way "remove" the danger by indicating its remoteness.

Stressing that you are all safe is comforting. Often, just your willingness to listen to their fears will help them.

The more honest you are in general in conversations with your children, the better-equipped they are to handle this sort of extreme situation. If you talk in euphemisms about death and prevent them from going to funerals, they will have a far different perception of reality than a child who knows that "Grandpa died," and can relate details of the funeral he attended. Honesty in advance pays off in extreme situations.

Understand that you are not sparing your children by lying to them either about death in general or the particulars of the situation. Stating a falsehood that your children must later unlearn is helpful to no one.

On the other hand, make sure that your comments are age appropriate. In the same way that you wouldn't share certain details of sex or money with younger children, you don't need to share all the details of terrorism.

Finally, do not use the euphemism "sleep" in referring to the dead. Otherwise you may well create a dread of bedtimes, with your child afraid that if he falls asleep, he may never awaken.

Convey a sense of hope

Regardless of the sadness of the particular situation, it's important that children retain a sense of hope and optimism about the world in general. Even in the most dire of circumstances, look for the silver lining in the clouds.

Stress the positives in the situation: Isn't it a lucky thing this happened when the Pentagon was under construction, and there weren't as many people there as usual? Wasn't that flight attendant brave in radioing down information during the hijacking?

Studies have shown that when the trauma involves human malevolency, rather than natural forces (such as accidents or hurricanes), children are affected more negatively, as are we all. So try to counteract this by looking at all the many examples of people going out of their way to help: Point out the many Americans giving blood and donations, the many foreigners showing support.

Encourage children to participate in something that will give the tragedy some meaning, or will actively help the victims: Go to a blood drive with your child, go to a prayer meeting or community support meeting, or take up a neighborhood collection to raise funds for the families.

"We collected $452 in one day!" one eight year old informed me gleefully. It was clear that being able to take action had lessened the impact of the situation for him, and given him renewed faith in the humanity of the people around him.

And whatever your personal convictions about the likelihood of another attack or more bad news, don't share these with your child. You need to be honest about facts and events that have occurred, but there is nothing for your child to gain from hearing your gloomy speculation. For that matter, it won't help you either: Think positive!

Be patient

Stressful situations require healing time. Be patient with your child, and be patient with yourself. Allow everyone the freedom to repeat the events of the experience as often as necessary.

"She keeps talking about it. Again and again," one mother told me. "It's as if she has to say it a certain amount of times—'And then the building fell down!'—'till she can get it out of her system. I wonder how long she'll be doing this. But I also realize that I'm spending a lot of time compulsively talking to neighbors about it. So maybe we all need that."

Stressful events that last a long time and pose a great threat, and where significant loss of life is involved, take longer to resolve than shorter, less intense situations.

And stressful situations that are clumped together—such as a series of terrorist attacks—are more disturbing still. Expect to spend more time than you might think healing.

A terrorist attack can loom large in the eyes of children. Give them the patient support and comfort they need to process the experience, again and again not just in the days after the attack, but in the weeks and months after as well. Children are extraordinarily resilient and they will heal eventually—but like any wound, it takes time.

Give them options

One thing children need in order to feel better after a terrorist incident is to recapture some of the power that the situation drained from them. Feeling helpless is an emotionally hazardous condition if it persists, and restoring your child's sense of empowerment is one of the easiest things you can do for them.

Since you're obviously unable to give them a sense of power over the events of the terrorism, enable them in other ways. Giving them options lets them feel they have some control over their lives and restores a sense of power over their daily existence.

Give them choices about what they'd like for dinner, or where they'd like to go for an outing. Ask them what they'd like to do during the weekend, whether they'd like to have a friend over, where you should go on a family outing or vacation. Even if your child is a toddler, you can let her pick her own outfit in the morning, or choose when to go to the park.

Another idea is to go through old family photo albums or their baby album, and point out all the different choices and decisions they've made throughout their lives. "See, here's where you wanted to go for your birthday party. Look, this is the dress you picked out – you wore it everyday for weeks!"

Reminding them of how much control they have over their lives and experiences will be subtly empowering and much appreciated.

Let them be helpful

Just as children respond well after a terrorist incident to choices, because they find it empowering, likewise children are comforted by helping out.

According to Mary Ann and James Emswiler, authors of "Guiding Your Child Through Grief," children report feeling comforted by helping out. Helping gives children a sense of self-esteem and a sense of control over a situation, and in that way it's quite empowering.

Helping out, like having options, gives your child a sense of control over the situation and their lives, control which a terrorist incident takes from them. In the aftermath of a terrorist situation, helping out can help your child reassert his feelings of control and power, and take back the situation.

"I thought it was a way of trying to make me feel better, but then I could see that the kids were helping set the table and cleaning up their stuff because it was making *them* feel better," said one astonished mother.

So even if your children don't ask for tasks—and many won't—look for opportunities for them to help. Ask them to fetch items from another part of the house for you. Have them help to entertain a younger sibling. Engage them in cleaning up or cooking with you.

Most children are happy to help in short doses anyway, because of the responsibility helping gives them. Particularly after a terrorist incident, it can be important in reestablishing their sense of control and empowerment. This is one case where helpful children are happy children.

Enhance their self esteem

Following a terrorist attack, it is useful for parents to remind their children about their strengths and skills. This will help to combat the helplessness that children often feel after a terrorist situation has ended.

Talk about what they do well and all the problems and difficult situations they have solved in the past. Remind them of their strengths and the many things over which they have mastery.

Again, this might be a good opportunity to pull out the old family photo albums and remind your child of how many things she has mastered over the years and how much she has learned. "Look, here's a picture of you tying your shoes. You were so happy when you figured out how to do that. Here's one of you learning to whistle. Here's a photo of you on your first pony ride."

Skills are a concrete manifestation of mastery over their lives, and children need to be reminded that they are not helpless, that they have expertise and power.

"I commented on how nicely Mary was learning to ride her bicycle," one mother noted. "I didn't think it was such a big deal, but she puffed up proudly and enumerated a whole list of other things she could do well. She was much cheerier the rest of the day."

It's important for children to feel some amount of control over themselves and their destinies, and the self esteem that goes along with it.

Make lists

Therapists who work with grief report that making lists can be therapeutic to those in mourning. Writing a list of things to do, for example, can be grounding and keep you focused. And writing lists can restore a sense of normalcy that is severely lacking following a terrorist incident or any other trauma. Finally, though you may feel emotionally fragile and exhausted, making a list can be energizing and uplifting.

Lists can also give children a sense of future and hope for "later" which can be lacking following a terrorist situation. Doing some concrete planning for later or even adult life can counteract their pessimism.

So make lists with your children of things you're grateful for, or happy about. Include talking to friends, music, playing with puppies, hugs, getting a birthday present, sitting in front of a woodstove, and playing on the beach.

And make lists of things connected to you and your child's future. Plan the details of a vacation. Prepare for an upcoming milestone birthday party. Make a to-do list of all the skills you want to learn or the places you want to go in the next five or ten years.

Make a fantasy list with your child of where they want to be when they are adults: Where they want to live, in what kind of a house, with how many children of their own, doing what sort of work, etc.

Make it a game and see who can come up with the largest and most interesting list of things that are good in your life. This is a fun activity even under normal circumstances; in the aftermath of a terrorist situation, it can be both grounding and cheering.

Maintain your children's behavior standards

In the aftermath of a terrorist attack, some children's behavior will disintegrate. Between the stress of hearing the news, the stress of watching adults falling apart, the children's change in routine, and the general climate of uneasiness, many children will find it difficult to follow the normal rules and maintain their usual standards of behavior.

On the one hand, you need to cut the kids a little slack: We're all a little stressed out, and you need to understand that children's behavior may suffer in subtle or not-so-subtle ways. This isn't the time to quibble over every little outburst or infraction.

On the other hand, you need to maintain the usual rules of the house and the usual expectations of your child.

"This is a very sad day, but we still need to do homework," one mother firmly told her children to their dismay.

Expectations are part of what makes your children's world secure. Don't upset their precarious sense of security even more by suddenly letting them do as they like. Continue to enforce household and family rules.

Some parents may find it easiest to be frank with their children: "I know this is a difficult time, and everything seems topsy-turvy," one mother confided to her three children. "But we're going to keep everything as normal as possible because it will make us all feel better. And that means that you're going to have to do all your regular things—like cleaning your room—and follow all the regular house rules—like going to bed at your regular time."

Altering behavior standards for terrorism situations will only serve to further unnerve your already anxious children: Keep to your regular rules and standards. Parental expectations are comforting.

Understand sleep patterns may change

Be aware that in the aftermath of a terrorist incident, sleep patterns are likely to change. Sleep is always affected by stress: Even going on vacation or having guests can result in sleepless nights. Children like their routines, and just the slightest change can affect their sleep patterns.

All the more so when the child has recently experienced a terrorist attack. Your child may be reluctant to go to sleep alone. He may want to snuggle into your bed or at least your bedroom. He may want more "tuck-ins" than usual, or ask you to check on him more often. His sleep patterns may change, resulting in later nights and earlier mornings.

You might well see an increase in nightmares, which can be terrifying for your child, as they can be interspersed with bits of the actual trauma situation. Or they may be peppered with his waking worries, and he may tell you he dreamed of losing you or being alone or in danger.

Even older children and teenagers may experience disruptions in their sleeping, or may feel scared about sleeping alone. You may hear older children who've been sleeping in attic rooms asking to return to the rooms of their childhood, or children who've been sleeping alone for years requesting a move to a room with siblings. Or your children may not be sleeping at all.

"They've been up all night for three nights running," said one exhausted mother. "I don't want them to move into our bedroom, but I'm wondering if that might make more sense than just spending the night running back and forth to them."

Be there for your child during his disturbed nights, and don't spend too much time worrying that things will never return to normal. Remember to show a lot of physical comfort during the day and before bedtime, be available to talk during waking hours, and above all exercise patience. This won't last forever.

Be alert for personality changes

In the same way that sleep patterns may change following the aftermath of a terrorism incident, you may see subtle, or not so subtle, personality changes in your child. In the aftermath of a single terrorist incident, these personality changes are unlikely to be permanent, but they may be worrisome nonetheless.

Your child's thoughts, attitudes, and relations to people may change. This can take all different forms: They may seem quieter or noisier, worried or silly, introverted or wild. You may see more aggressive play, more anxiety about strangers, or louder and more boisterous behavior.

In teenagers you may see more cynicism or sarcasm. You are also likely to notice them taking a sudden intense interest in world events and the news, as a way of keeping a sense of control over the situation.

But even very young children can be affected by the upheaval of basic expectations about their world.

"My five year old just became much quieter than usual. Very shy, very timid, very silent. As though he was suddenly tentative about his life," one mother told us.

You may see an erosion of your child's trust in the goodness of people. You may experience your child's decreased feelings of safety. You may see selfish, preoccupied behavior, suspicion, or pessimism.

See it for what it is, and don't dwell on it: It's likely to be temporary. Envelope your child in warmth and love.

Watch for anger

Among the personality changes or new attitudes that you might see in your child following a terrorist incident is sudden or increased anger. Unless the anger is harmful to your child or others, this can be a very healing emotion, although it may be difficult to live with.

Keep in mind that anger, in particular, can be a cover for other, more complicated emotions. If you notice that your child seems unusually angry, or is behaving more aggressively than is usual, there's a good chance that she feels scared and helpless.

"I came downstairs the next morning," said one mother, "and Bobbie was jumping up and down on his favorite stuffed bear. I didn't know whether to laugh or cry."

Remember to comfort your child often, whether he seems to need it or not. "Tough" emotions may just be a cover for real fear and concern. Or it may not be a cover for anything—it may simply be anger. Give frequent hugs, and be available to talk to your child.

Parents often find it difficult to see their children expressing anger. Our tendency is to distract them or rebuke them. Forcing your child to contain his emotions, however, is the worst thing you can do if you want to move past the incident.

As long as the anger is not harmful to the child or others, it is a positive thing. Remember that any expression of emotion, including anger, is a healing, empowering experience.

So watch your child's anger without reprimand, and show your love and comfort in as many ways as you can.

Listen for complaints of bruises

You might not think that your child's sudden preoccupation with a skinned knee is related to a terrorist incident—but you'd be wrong.

Worries of bumps or bruises, or complaints of pain or fatigue are all stress or trauma reactions. Particularly for a child who finds it difficult—because of age or emotional development—to verbalize his emotional fragility or fear, complaints of bruising can be a way of attracting parental attention for a hurt that is not actually physical.

Your child may exhibit a sudden new concern about her cut knees and skinned shins, or react disproportionately to a minor bump. She may complain of tummy ache or headache. She may experience rashes, lethargy, nausea, colds, weakness, forgetfulness, or cramps. Be alert for such talk particularly if your child is usually not a complainer.

"Andy kept whining about the cut on his knee. He's scraped that knee up bicycling every week of his life and I've never heard him talk about it before," wondered one father.

These complaints are a way for your child to say, "I'm hurting inside" without the necessity of vocalizing it. Younger children may take this tact because of the difficulty in verbalizing their complicated emotions; older children may exhibit the same symptoms because of embarrassment of discussing what's really bothering them. Or they may complain of bruising or pain without understanding that they're really experiencing emotional fragility and anxiety.

Either way, take their concerns seriously and comfort their tears. Even if the hurt strikes you as a minor nothing, be aware that it probably masks a deeper emotional wound, and tend to it accordingly.

Such physical manifestations may continue long after the initial attack. Listen to the complaints, and be appropriately sympathetic. By comforting the alleged physical manifestation of what is actually a psychological internal hurt, you'll be healing both.

Watch for recklessness and carelessness

Another manifestation of the aftermath of terrorism is daredevil behavior and recklessness. It's unclear whether the child is acting this way in despair at the situation, or whether it's an attempt at self-injury so they can be returned to the safety of their mother.

In fact, children who are engaging in such incautious behavior may themselves be unaware of what they are doing.

If you see your child preparing to jump out of a tree or engage in other unusual, risky behavior, take precautions. And if you see a pattern of such behavior, get professional counseling for your child at once.

Be alert for overly detailed fears

If your child's worries about the situation seem particularly graphic and realistic to you, take note.

According to Dr. Lenore Terr, author of "Too Scared to Cry: How trauma affects children…and ultimately us all," once a fear sounds very literal and very specific there is a strong possibility that actual experience underlies the fear.

She notes that while many developing youngsters develop a fear of dogs, they fear all of them—not just large ones with white spots. If the fear is that specific, it is likely to be the result of a specific experience.

If your child's details of terrorism while playing or in conversation sound too real to you, or in some way too graphic or explicit, try to initiate a conversation with your child to get at the underlying fear.

It is possible that your child misunderstood something he heard on the radio or in the schoolyard, and that his fear stems from something that you might be able to put to rest. Young children, in particular, are quite capable of misunderstanding the conversations and news reports they hear—which may make the situation more frightening than it need be.

In any case, discussing the details of the situation, if your child is already aware of them anyway, will help to soften the reality. And parental participation in discussing the fear will probably make it less scary for your child.

So talk it through with your child—and talk it through again, as often as necessary.

Don't downplay the trauma to your child

One thing almost every parent succumbs to, in the aftermath of a trauma such as a terrorist incident, is the inclination to play down the effects of the terrorism to her child.

It is tempting for parents to conclude, after the immediate situation is over, that their child hasn't suffered from the incident.

"After all," one mother told me, "She wasn't actually *in* the terrorist attack! She just heard about it on television like everyone else. Why is she going on about it all the time? You'd think she was actually there!"

Surprisingly, research has shown that mere witnesses to a violent or traumatic event are actually more likely to turn violent in the future as a result of their experience than the primary victims of the attack. It is, in fact, the mere bystanders who are most adversely affected. And that means that your child, who thankfully was *not* directly involved in the situation, can be most affected.

Moreover, those who were not physically present at the event can be as emotionally harmed as those who were there, according to other studies.

So your child who *only* saw the incident on television may be as wounded emotionally as had she been physically present during the attack.

By processing their feelings and receiving the comfort of their loved ones after witnessing such an event, you can reduce the likelihood of permanent scarring. So treat your child's intensity around the events seriously.

Take some time without the kids

Make sure you spend some time processing your own feelings about the events, without your children around.

A terrorist incident is frightening for adults, as well as children. You may fear for your own personal safety, and that of your family. You may experience the same feelings of panic and anxiety that you need to look for in your child.

A terrorist situation may also renew old feelings of loss or bereavement that you need to work through. It may bring back an adult's feelings of terror that were experienced in a war. It may bring feelings of loss that were experienced after the death of a loved one. Or it may bring other, seemingly unrelated memories, needs, or emotional hurts from childhood that should be resolved.

You need to spend some time resolving those feelings of grief when you are not in the presence of your children.

That might mean going for a walk by yourself just to think about things, keeping a journal, or talking about the situation with a friend or a therapist.

In addition, couples need to spend time with each other. The stress of a terrorist attack can have detrimental effects on family relationships if not carefully managed, and you don't want to put further stress on your children by adding the burden of forcing them to listen to your fighting.

So spend some time together doing something fun or relaxing. Take a walk, play a board game, read aloud to each other. Try not to spend all the time discussing the situation. Do *not* spend your time together listening to the news!

Listen for the aftershocks

After the tragedy, pay careful attention to your child's behavior. Is she moody? More lethargic than usual? Poorly behaved? Eating less? Listless?

Any of these symptoms might be a clue that she was very shaken by this incident and needs to process it more completely.

Try doing something active together: Plant a garden, take a jog, go on a hike. Encouraging your children to express themselves through art, music, drama, puppetry, or writing can be a way for children to make themselves heard, and is often less threatening to children than verbalizing what they're feeling.

On the other hand, when a parent's worry about a child's reaction to a terrorist incident is excessive, the parent's very anxiety can overwhelm the child with despair. Don't burden your child with fears that are unnecessary. Take a one-day-at-a-time approach, and try not to worry compulsively about your child unless it seems warranted.

Watch for withdrawal

Be alert for signs that your child is withdrawing from the world. For your child, the world used to be a safe, secure place. Suddenly, the world has become scary. And faced with a suddenly scary world, withdrawal may seem the safest approach to your child. It is, above all, fear of being further (unhappily) surprised by more bad news that your child wants to avoid.

Some children will try to make the world feel safer by holding back on their activities: Avoiding rough play, distancing from classmates, and abdicating from any activities that might trigger a memory of the incident are all ways of withdrawing. And by withdrawing, your child lessens the chance that she will be surprised again by something scary. This fear of future fear can immobilize children.

"It's as if she's withholding herself from the world now that it's proven itself to be an unsafe place," one father said sadly. "I long for the old rough-and-tumble interactions."

Encourage your child gradually to participate in her former activities. Don't lecture, but do provide gentle support.

Ultimately, your child needs to realize that her behavior and activities will not affect the world situation or her personal situation, and that resuming her normal routines will not put her at additional risk of trauma.

But this is something that's more easily preached than practiced. So be encouraging, and be patient.

But don't look for school problems

Although you may notice changes of all sorts in your child following a terrorism experience, the one that you probably won't see is deteriorating performance in school.

Studies, both of recent immigrant children who had experienced traumatic situations, and of kidnapped children, reveal that traumatic situations do not usually have a negative effect on school performance.

Even a psychically traumatized child can work hard in school, behave normally in school, and get grades consistent with their performance before the trauma.

School is an organizing structure, so the fact that kids do ok in school isn't surprising. Under most circumstances, children will keep it together at school—and then fall apart at home, where it's "safe" to do so.

Consistently, do not assume that your child is *not* affected just because their school behavior and performance has remained stable.

Asking your child's teacher for opinions on whether the situation has unduly affected your child, therefore, is insufficient, because your child may not be exhibiting the extent of his uneasiness at school—only at home.

In such situations, it is more likely to be children's *home* behaviors that are an indicator of problems, not school behaviors.

So watch what is happening at home.

Watch for regression

Watch your child for behavioral regression.

Children under stress typically respond with a temporary lapse in age-appropriate behavior. In the same way that bringing a newborn into the house may mean your three year old is suddenly back in diapers, in the aftermath of a terrorist attack you may find all your children behaving suddenly younger than their ages.

Regression is one way for upset children to cope. You may see thumb sucking, toilet accidents, and the like.

By returning to a younger stage, your child is forcing you to respond as when the child was younger and needier.

"He's suddenly wetting his bed at night and he's been toilet trained for years," one mother worried.

This is a natural response to stress, and for many children, an inevitable one. Respond by treating the child as if he *were* the younger age he is attempting to recapture, and provide lots of extra love and warmth.

And don't worry: This behavior won't last forever.

Watch for denial

Confronted with a single, horrifying event, adults often react with denial, whereby they consciously prevent themselves from thinking about the incident, and disbelieve its reality.

Children, on the other hand, faced with a single traumatic event, remember the horror with clarity.

However, confronted with numerous instances of disaster, or a series of horrors, a child will brace for shock and start ignoring the reality. Repeated disasters encourage denial in children. And denial—under certain circumstances such as these—is not necessarily an unhealthy thing.

If your child is in denial about terrorism, and refuses to admit that anything bad happened, he may have been strongly affected by the circumstances, and you may need to watch him carefully to make sure he's recovering.

But just because he's not talking about it doesn't mean that he's in denial: It's also possible that it just hasn't appeared on his radar screen.

If your child seems unaffected by events, uninterested in discussing the situation, and generally immune to what's going on around him, don't assume there's a problem. Make note of it, and pay attention to see if anything further develops over time.

Watch for fear of the future

Children who have been affected by a scary event, such as a terrorist incident, may express concerns about all sorts of things, and exhibit all sorts of out-of-the-ordinary behavior.

Even if your child is expressing concerns about lack of a future—or if questioned, cannot seem to conceive of having a future—don't worry. Fear of future is likely to be just a temporary reaction to such a situation.

"After the terrorist attack, it seemed that Carla stopped making plans. She didn't want to talk about the future at all—going to college, getting married, having kids. She suddenly seemed unconfident that she would *have* a future," said one mother.

If your child suddenly doesn't seem able to envision her future, assume that her reaction is a temporary response to the immediate events, and will fade in time.

Much more worrisome than a temporary inability to plan for the future is a chronic hopelessness or despair that would indicate a serious depression.

If your child's hopelessness continues, monitor her closely; if it does not disappear over time, and your child seems to be falling into a prolonged depression, seek counseling.

Get professional help

If your child is generally resilient and able to cope with emotionally challenging situations, she will be more likely to bounce back after a terrorist attack. If you have a child who finds such situations challenging in general, he may be more at risk after a terrorist attack.

Be aware that there is an anxiety condition called posttraumatic stress disorder that can occur after witnessing a terrifying event. In adults, the condition can cause flashbacks and frightening memories of the traumatic event.

In children, it is more likely to manifest as obsessive play about the incident. This disorder can and does occur to children who have seen violent imagery on television: It is not necessary that they actually have been in the situation themselves.

According to the American Psychological Association, "Continued and aggressive emotional outbursts, serious problems at school, preoccupation with the traumatic event, continued and extreme withdrawal, and other signs of intense anxiety or emotional difficulties all point to the need for professional assistance."

Bear in mind that symptoms can often erupt months after the event. If you suspect your child's behavior is posttraumatic stress disorder, seek counseling.

Support groups may also be useful to children who do not seem to be recovering after an incident of terrorism. Often, just realizing that others are still caught in the same morass of feelings can be helpful to children and adults alike.

Take the high moral ground

In the aftermath of a terrorist incident, it is incredibly tempting to blame the perpetrators and rail against them.

Nonetheless, whatever you feel about the suspected religious or ethnic identities of the terrorists, avoid your inclination to comment. Your child will only be more confused if you share hateful feelings about a particular group.

"I know other parents who jumped on the blame bandwagon," said a mother of two. "But I'm glad that I didn't. I don't want my children to learn to think that way, and I don't want them to grow up perpetuating those ideas."

Childhood trauma can instigate a generalized anger focused (rationally or not) on one single category of people.

Don't compound this tendency in your child by singling out a group for your anger. You don't want your child to go through life saddled with a burning anger against a particular group of people. Political situations change, and political foes and friends swap sides. Creating or foster resentment or hatred in your child against an ethnic group is not productive.

And studies have shown that lack of empathy is the key trait that terrorists and violent criminals share. Don't exhibit your biases to your children, and try to cultivate empathy in them so that they grow up to be empathic, caring adults.

Give them something higher to cling to

Don't let terrorism shatter your child's faith—be it in God, or in humankind. If you believe in God, admit that it's hard to know how to reconcile that with a tragedy of this proportion. Tell your child that sometimes human nature is baffling and incomprehensible.

And belief in God does not necessarily mean that you always understand why God does what he does.

"We compared it to the Holocaust. We know God is there—but sometimes we don't understand why he allows what he allows," said one mother. "It's not a great answer, but it's hard to reconcile God with so much evil."

Admit your confusion and sadness, but don't forget to point out the good things, the silver lining, and the shows of support and valor that are all around us in trying times.

If you have any affiliation with a church or synagogue, now is a great time to pursue that. Sharing such a situation with a community of like-minded people can be incredibly supportive and comforting, for both your child and you.

Don't attempt to feed your child platitudes about God unless you believe them; he won't be fooled if you're sprouting a party line that you don't believe.

But don't allow your own doubts and skepticism to prevent your child from being comforted, either. God means different things to different people, and your child may very well find solace in a God that watches over him personally, whether or not you truly believe in a personal God.

Don't forget to take care of yourself

One of the problems inherent in extreme national trauma such as a terrorist attack is that parents, deluged with concern for their children, forget that they themselves also underwent the trauma.

"I'm so worried about Emma; I'm only focused on that. I'm exhausted," one mom confided.

Don't neglect your child, but don't neglect yourself either. You are also shaken, worried, and depressed. We all are. And we all need some extra love and comfort for the days ahead.

Expect less of yourself in the next days. You may feel tired, lethargic, and unable to accomplish anything. You may feel exhausted and sleep-deprived. Don't worry if you feel distracted and unable to cope. These are natural outcomes and will be alleviated over time.

And don't forget to take care of yourself. Try to get enough sleep, and try to eat well-balanced regular meals. Reach out to people more than you might normally—stop and talk to the neighbors; call friends who are long-distance. Fostering a sense of community during difficult times makes us all feel less alone.

And remember to stop and smell the roses.

In the wake of a terrorist attack it's human nature to feel survivor guilt and attempt to curtail your pleasures. But happiness isn't a betrayal of those who died. Glory in the wonder of being alive, and enjoy it with your child, family, and community.

Relish the positives

Ironically, some parents will find that the aftermath of a terrorist incident or other trauma can be a positive thing. It's hard to believe, but it can be true: Trauma can sometimes clarify your priorities.

One mother noted, "It sounds ridiculous, but having seen great tragedy, I'm now less worried about the little inconveniences of life. Behavior problems, traffic jams— everything seems less important than the sanctity of our family life, which is wonderful. It's not that the terrorism was good—it certainly wasn't. But we're seeing our lives with clearer vision now."

So take the opportunity the situation affords to spend more time together as a family, let go of the minor nuisances, and cherish the important things in life.

Tailoring Your Approach to the Age of Your Child

Before you begin answering children's questions about terrorism, you need to think carefully about the developmental level of your child. Children understand events at their level and through the lens of their experiences. As parents, we need to talk to our children openly, honestly, but in a way that will help them understand what they need to know—without unnecessarily frightening them.

Approach conversations about terrorism with your children in the same way that you would approach conversations about sex and money: Certain information is appropriate for certain ages.

Infants

Although infants are pre-verbal, they are intuitively aware of the emotions of the people around them. They will notice instantly that you are smiling less, playing differently or not at all, and generally not there for them in your usual way. Infants whose parents are upset have difficult eating and sleeping; have a tendency to cry more; and are generally "fussier" than usual. In the aftermath of a terrorist attack, your infant will certainly pick up on your emotions.

As much as possible, soothe your infant by keeping him close. Keep to his regular schedule, and try to make up in physical solace what you are unable to give in emotional constancy. Expect your infant to be as irritable and emotionally fragile as everyone else in the family during these difficult days, and be patient.

Preschoolers

Preschoolers, though verbal, are obviously too young to appreciate the political significance of a terrorist attack. At this age, children are only interested in the world as it relates to their own experiences. They will be particularly interested in the sights that they understand—the firemen, the buildings crashing, the airplanes diving. They don't have much of an understanding of death at this age, and often think of it as a temporary condition.

"After we lit a memorial candle for the victims of a terrorist attack, my son said he wanted to watch until the candle burned down all the way. When I asked why, he told me that when the candle was gone, the dead people would come back to life."

Because he doesn't understand that death is a permanent condition, your preschooler may not understand why everyone is so sad.

You need to make sure your preschooler knows what's happening to some extent, because he is sure to hear about a major terrorist incident even if you don't personally tell him. On the other hand, if he doesn't ask, you don't need to tell them all the dismaying details. Simply say something like, "There was a big accident and a lot of people were hurt." If he asks for further details, provide them, but be sure you are only answering his questions rather than giving him more information than he needs.

You will probably find that your preschooler will want to talk about what happened again and again. Let him. Healing will occur faster for an upset child if he is able to continue to rehash the situation. Drawing, drama, and writing can be helpful as well; see the chapter *Writing, Drawing, and Playing as Therapy* for more information on using these activities as therapy.

When listening to news reports of the violence, be sure to assure your child that your emotional reaction and anger have nothing to do with him. Children of this age feel guilt for a great many things, and if they see your anger they may assume it's directed towards them. Cuddle your preschooler in your lap while listening to the news so that he is comforted and realize your anger is directed elsewhere.

Elementary school children

Six to twelve year olds are at a developmental level that enables them to understand events outside their direct experience, though they still will have little grasp of the political significance. You need to be especially honest with your child of this age: She is old enough to access the information elsewhere (by interrogating other children on the playground, for example) yet still be confused about motivations and implications of terrorism.

A simple explanation for this age group is probably best. Try something like, "Something terrible happened today. There was an accident at some buildings in New York, and many people were hurt." Explain that that's why you've been listening to the radio so much. Stress that your family is safe. Then wait for her to ask you questions. You might also want to talk to her about positive steps you will take, such as donating blood to people who need it, or raising money to help the people in the attack.

Although they technically understand death, children under the age of about nine think that death is something that only happens to old people. Thus, the reality of hearing about younger people's deaths may disturb them, or they may not internalize it. A slightly older child will understand that death is possible even for younger people, and will be aware of his own mortality, though usually he will be in denial about this.

Remember, also, to reassure children that their schools are safe, and that the rest of the family will be safe during the school day while they are at school.

Teenagers

Teenagers will be getting a lot of their information about a terrorist incident from outside the home. They are also at a developmental level sufficient to understand the political significance of the event. Finally, teens will realize that there is a possibility of further violence in a way that a younger child will not.

Despite the fact that your teenagers may already know about the situation, make sure you process it with them. Talk to them and allow time in the next weeks for them to talk to you. Don't assume that they don't need to talk about it and that they're handling their emotions well. Some adolescents may be scared to discuss the situation, some may seem fine and uninterested in the discussion, and others will be brash in their assurances that they are not scared, but fear is at the root of all of these responses. Find the time to talk.

Answering Children's Questions

Mommy, what happened?

Start by hugging your child. When she says she wants to know what happened, what she's really asking for is to be protected from the scary events, and to be safe.

Tell her that you don't know exactly what happened. It's the truth: A lot of the initial information in terrorism reports is just plain wrong, and is later rescinded; point that out to your child. (That's the downside of listening to the news as it is happening; the news is a lot more accurate, as well as a lot more bearable, well after the event.)

Do say that people were hurt if that much is clear, and that you are sad. Your child will certainly realize that you are upset, and it's better for her to hear it from you directly.

Make sure she realizes that your anger and grief are not directed at her, however. Cuddle and comfort her physically so she internalizes that.

As events unfold, you can give your child more information, as much as you think is age-appropriate. But don't overburden her with more than she really asks to know. And keep her close and cuddled: By asking you questions, children are really seeking reassurance that they are safe and protected.

Will we all die?

Keep in mind that *how* you answer this question is as important as what you say. If your child senses that you are terrified and out of control, she won't believe your verbal reassurance. Try to aim for sadness, rather than despair.

Stress that your family is safe. That's really what your child is most concerned about: Death of strangers, especially if your children are sheltered from watching the visual images on television, is not nearly as disturbing to children as upsetting the sanctity of their loved ones.

If the events happened in a distant locale, explain how far away that is in a way even your littlest child can understand: "It would take us 45 days to walk from here to there. That's very far away."

If your child and family believes in God or another higher being, you can tell your child that it is your job as a parent to keep her safe, and it is God's job to keep your whole family and community safe.

Now is a good time to revive your synagogue or church affiliation if that is something that might give your family comfort during this time.

If your family is unaffiliated religiously, a spiritual or community group that feels similarly to you might be worth looking into. It's important for everyone, children and adults alike, to have the support of a community during such difficult days.

Why do people have to die, anyway?

Explain to your child that everything living is born and then dies: Dying is a natural part of living.

Plants grow and then die; animals live and then die; and people live and eventually die. As the Bible says, "To everything there is a season."

Comfort your children with the thought that most people die when they get to be really, really old.

There are several excellent books on death and dying geared to children of all different ages. The best of these are listed at the end of this book.

When your child asks this question, he isn't really asking a metaphysical question anyway. What he really wants to know is why people *he* knows and is close to have to die, and whether anyone he knows and loves is likely to die.

Try to reassure your child that it is unlikely that anyone he knows and loves will be involved in a terrorist incident. Remind him that it is your job to keep your family safe, and that you will do that.

What does dying feel like?

Tell your child that we can't really know that, since it hasn't happened to us, and the people who have died (use an example if you have one: "like Aunt Sophie") can't tell us.

If you wish, relate stories of what people who have almost died thought they saw: Lights, a tunnel, loved family members coming to greet them. If you practice a religion that has a perspective on death, this might be a good time to introduce that.

Gloss over the details of terrorism's horror with a younger child and, if asked, say that death usually happens quickly and peacefully.

Remember that younger children often don't understand a lot of what they are hearing on the news anyway. This can either make them more or less fearful and upset, depending on what they think has happened.

My 5 year old, hearing that something had burned down, happily told me that he was glad the fire had burned down, "because if it had burned up, someone might have gotten hurt!"

If you hear a happy misinterpretation of this sort, and there's no older child to set them straight, it might be best to let well enough alone.

In any case, when asked about death, explain that people who die usually look relaxed and peaceful, and don't seem to be in pain.

Why did this happen?

This is one of the hardest questions to answer, because it means, to some extent, the end of your child's innocence.

Children are born trusting the world. In the aftermath of a terrorist attack, when your child asks why, you will have to convey to her that the world isn't always a safe place.

Tell your child that there are some horrible people in the world. Stress that there aren't very many—you don't want her to feel more scared than she has to. But explain that every so often, there's a horrible person who does some terrible thing.

If your child is old enough to know any history, you might take this opportunity to talk about other horrible people who have lived in the past, such as Hitler. The underlying message is that sometimes, terrible people do terrible things.

If your child has had any positive experiences with the police (some children are scared of policemen) you can explain that we have policemen (and governments, laws, and jails) to protect citizens from these few horrible people.

The important thing is to make sure the child understands that most people are good and behave nicely to each other, and that horrible people are rare.

Be sure you use the word "horrible" or "terrible" in referring to the perpetrators, rather than the word "bad." Your children may have been called "bad" after being naughty and you need to draw a strong distinction for them between being somewhat mischievous and being a terrorist!

Children would much rather feel guilty than powerless, as long as they can maintain some sense of control over a situation. Thus, in the aftermath of a terrorist situation, they may feel it is their fault, particularly if they hear the terrorists referred to as "bad." Make sure you draw the distinction for them.

Will it happen here?

When your child asks if terrorism will happen here, he wants to know if he'll be safe, and if your family will be safe.

Strangers are too distant a concept for him to worry about: He's concerned about his own family and friends.

Remind your child that until now, nothing bad has ever happened where you live, if that's true. Tell your child that in general, such terrible things hardly ever happen.

Try something like, "For hundreds of years, we've been safe living here."

Children don't really appreciate the unlikelihood of such an event occurring, but the reassurance in your voice when you say this will be helpful to them anyway.

And if you couch it in more personal terms that is still better:

"Grandma and Grandpa grew up here and nothing bad happened here; I grew up here and nothing bad happened; and I don't think anything bad will happen here."

Keep reminding your child that it is your job, as a parent, to make sure they stay safe. "Mommy and Daddy will do everything we have to keep us all safe and happy."

Is there going to be a war here?

Tell your child the truth: No one knows if there is going to be a war here. We all hope not. But nobody knows for sure.

Tell her: The important thing is that we're going to keep you and our whole family safe.

If you have family members or close friends serving in the armed forces, you can say, "Uncle Frank is going to help protect our country and keep us safe."

Make sure your child understands that even though you hope war will not occur here, you and your family will be prepared for whatever happens. If you have made emergency plans or preparations, share these with your child.

"When Rena asked whether there would be a war, I showed her all the supplies we had laid on in the basement," shared one mother. "We talked about having warm jackets for winter, and army rations that were portable in case we needed to go somewhere suddenly. I showed her the duffel bags we had packed with emergency medical supplies in case we needed them. We also talked about what we might do to meet up if we became separated from my husband.

"I think just being aware of the fact that we had made plans and were on top of the situation was comforting to her."

Will any bombs fall on us?

Tell your child that in the entire history of America, since your great, great, great, great, great grandfather was alive, no bombs have fallen on your town. (This statement is true for almost everyplace in the United States mainland; there are only a very few places that were bombed during the Japanese attack in World War II.)

Reiterate that you will keep your child and family safe.

In the event that war actually erupts in the U.S., tell your child that you have a safe place to go if it becomes necessary, where bombs cannot land (that is, a bomb shelter).

You might want to tell your young child that going to the safe place will be like a camping trip, and you will bring food, sleeping bags, and favorite toys with you. Remind her that your whole family will be together.

This question may take other forms, particularly as events unfold and depending on the age of your child. Basically, these questions are all the same.

You may hear your child ask whether we are at danger of exposure to chemical or biological weapons; whether you are worried about water or air contamination; whether you think we are at risk of being the victims of germ warfare; whether there is going to be a war on U.S. soil.

In all these cases, reiterate the basic point: That you will do your best to keep your family safe, and how you are making plans to do so. If you have an older child, and are taking precautions with which he can help, by all means involve him in the preparations: Helping to organize bottled water (or emergency supplies, or whatever the situation warrants) will be empowering and make him feel better about what's going on.

What about anthrax and smallpox?

Your child may ask about anthrax or smallpox, or other scary situations that may be bandied about in the news.

One of the most difficult parts of this unfolding situation is that whatever you say to reassure your child today, it may be totally untrue by tomorrow. In September of 2001 it was inconceivable that our air safety was at such risk. A few weeks later we were denying that anthrax could be spread so easily. Then we worried about smallpox and nuclear weapons. And who knows what next week will bring?

Rather than trying to comfort your child's fears by reassuring them with "truths" that might be disproven, try instead to reassure them that you're their parent; that it's your job to take care of them; and that whatever the situation brings, you'll be there for them.

Older children may want to argue that you're unable to predict what will happen, or that it will be impossible to keep them safe, if, for example, a smallpox epidemic should begin. For the child who is old enough to understand, it's ok to say that you don't know what will happen, the situation is volatile and no one can know, but that you will take care of them as best you can.

Think of this as an opportunity to show your children how to react healthily to life's curveballs. Encourage them to join you in community action or to work off some of the strain by exercising together. Model good responses to stress for them—it will be good for both of you.

Are there any terrorists here?

Tell your child that terrorists usually come from far-away parts of the world. Some countries have a lot of terrorism, but not the United States.

Reassure your child that the government, the police, and the military work hard to keep terrorists out of our country, and catch any who slip in.

For an older child, point to the news reports of terrorists being tracked down and deported. Since many older children and teenagers will want to control their fear by becoming news addicts and being very up on the politics of the situation anyway, they will know that steps are being taken to rid the country of the problem.

Again, remind your child that you will keep them and your family safe.

With a younger child, you may find that this question takes a slightly different form. Instead of asking directly about terrorists, your preschool child may worry about burglars or robbers. She may suddenly become scared again about evil monsters under the beds or in the dark corners of your house, or she may complain about ghosts or other scary characters that are suddenly lurking in your home.

Understand that all these fears are coming from the same place, and comfort your child accordingly.

What should I do if I see a terrorist?

Reassure your child that he won't be seeing any terrorists. Remind him that it is the job of policemen, soldiers, and the FBI to catch dangerous criminals, including terrorists.

Despite the fact that you know your child won't be meeting terrorists anytime soon, you might want to engage in a "What If" scenario game which can be comforting to some children.

If you do this, make sure you keep it lighthearted and fun, rather than grim and depressed. Tell your child that you would throw your infant's dirty diapers at the terrorist, and then fling your butterfly net over their heads. The more fantastic and humorous a response you can conjure, the better.

One mother who played this fantasy game with her eight year old thought it helped his spirits immensely. "We were talking about what to do if we were on a plane that got hijacked, and I said I'd toss my airline meal at the terrorist, and since it was made of rubber anyway, it would bean him in the head and he'd never get up. My eight year old was howling with laughter for hours."

Again remind your child that you will keep her safe. This sounds like a broken record, but it is truly the most important thing you can do. The physical comfort of your embrace, and promise to keep her protected, is what she is asking you for.

Did this happen because I was bad?

Children often feel guilty about events that have nothing to do with them. After a parent's divorce, they may feel their sibling fighting was responsible; after the death of a loved one they may feel it was because of the time they said they hated him.

Perhaps because children are scolded by parents frequently, when a traumatic event occurs, they may feel it was somehow their responsibility or fault for not behaving better.

What a child least wants to feel is powerless. Children want to feel that they are in control of a situation. If the choice comes down to feeling guilty (because somehow their bad behavior caused the situation) or feeling powerless, children will almost always opt for guilt.

So although your child wants to hear the reassurance that he had nothing to do with this, he is simultaneously hoping it was his fault, so that he was somehow in control of the situation.

Try explaining to your child: "Sometimes bad things happen, but it's not your fault." And then empower him in other ways—by giving him more control over his environment, or more choices that are usually not open to him, to alleviate his feelings of powerlessness.

Can I stay home from school?

The day after a terrorist attack, if your child says he doesn't want to go to school, or claims a headache or sore throat, ask directly if he is afraid because of what happened.

If your child is distressed, keep him home for the day or part of the day. Ask if it would help if you drove him to school, or picked him up at the end. For teenagers it might be more helpful to be in school where they can process the situation with their peers.

Separation anxiety following a terrorist attack is a natural and common response. The younger the child, the more likely he is to express this. Parents may see clingy behavior, resistance to babysitters, and unwillingness to leave for school.

Trauma can temporarily destroy a child's previous feelings of safety; by refusing to separate, she is able to rely on the physical presence of her trusted family. Be sensitive to it, and don't push.

Occasionally, an extremely upset child may be reluctant to venture outside the house at all. On the one hand, this phobia helps the child feel more in control of the situation, because she can avoid being exposed to further trauma in what has become, to her, a scary world.

On the other hand, even this extreme reaction will not relieve her fear.

Staying at home to avoid further trauma is ultimately unsuccessful, since even inside the house a traumatized child will feel helpless and terrified, be it during the day or in nightmares.

If this problem continues, seek professional counseling for your child.

Is it ok to cry?

Most children won't ask this directly. Some children, in fact, evince worry by denying their fear, and loudly proclaiming their bravery.

These children are often the ones who, in the privacy of their bedrooms at night, experience terrific nightmares. The more vehement they are about their power, the more aggressive they are in their play, the more likely they are to experience an underlying fearfulness.

From children around the age of eight, especially, you may hear this question about crying guised in the form of doubt or scorn for someone who has exhibited the behavior:

"Davey was a crybaby when he heard the radio today," a friend's 7-year-old related to his father.

What he is really asking is permission to express this feeling himself, and assurance that it is an acceptable way to deal with the situation.

Give the assurance. "Crying is ok. That doesn't mean that Davey is a coward. Brave people cry when they're sad. I cried yesterday when I heard the news. Sometimes crying can help make you feel better."

Is it ok to laugh and smile?

In the same way that some children won't be able to cry without permission, others won't be able to enjoy themselves.

Survivor guilt is a very powerful emotion, and even very young children may feel it.

Tell your child: "It seems like the whole country is so sad right now, and you may feel funny if you find yourself laughing and having a good time as if nothing happened. But you shouldn't feel funny about it. People are resilient, and that's what makes us people."

You may also find that both you and your child go through moments of denial, where you temporarily forget the entire situation. When you catch yourself engaging happily in normal activity, you may feel guilt.

You shouldn't. This intermittent denial is healthy, and encourages healing.

Persuade your child to go on with his life. Play games, read books, spend time together happily as a family.

Don't make the mistake of censuring a child who is having fun, even if it is in the midst of the news coverage. You can't regulate sadness, and shouldn't.

What can we do to make a difference?

Even young children may ask you if there isn't something that they can do to help. People of all ages want to feel that they can make a difference, and do something helpful.

And of course they can, and doing it is guaranteed to make them feel better.

Younger children can tie a black armband on, or a yellow ribbon around a tree, or help in lowering the flag to half-mast.

They can help you in planting a tree in memory of the people who died. They can draw a picture or write a letter in memory of the dead, or to mail to the families.

You can all light a memorial candle together, and say a prayer if that is your inclination. Better yet, you can organize a neighborhood event to do this with others.

Older children can join you in donating to a blood drive, or canvassing the neighbors to raise funds for the victims' families. You and your children can attend a prayer service or a memorial service.

Taking positive action will counteract feelings of helplessness and promote faster healing. Doing something helpful is empowering, and wonderfully helpful.

Why am I having bad dreams?

Children often react to terrorism by shutting it out of their mind as much as they can. Particularly in the event of multiple traumatic events over an extended period of time, children may find it easier to block the events from their waking hours.

It's a coping mechanism: Having dreams is the way we digest and process our life experiences. But the trauma will surface in phobias, nightmares, or other undesirable symptoms or behaviors.

There's no wonder cure for bringing your child's fears out into the open to protect her from nightmares other than processing her emotions during waking hours.

If your child complains of nightmares, try explaining it this way:

"Sometimes you have bad dreams when you've seen something scary or sad, even if you decide to never think about it again. If there's something that's scaring you, we can talk about it. Talking about it might help to make the bad dreams go away. It may take a while."

You might try planning with your child what he should dream; sometimes discussing what the content of his dreams could be will help. Or you might try physically chasing the tigers out from under the bad, or throwing the bad dreams out the open window.

Recognize that, in the aftermath of a terrorist situation it will take time till the nightmares lessen. And particularly when the situation is ongoing, your child may continue to experience nightmares for a while.

Why do I keep thinking about it?

Following a terrorist incident, children frequently experience undesired, usually visual, memories of the event: Fragments flying, people screaming, towers tumbling, enter as random images at random times.

The intrusion of such imagery is incredibly traumatic and insistent, and your child may experience panic. Certainly it is difficult for many children to banish these visual images, and very hard to stop thinking about the situation.

Tell your child that the more you talk about the event together, the less he'll think about it when he's not with you.

Over time, the memories of the event will begin to fade, and eventually he won't have to think about it much at all.

Will I ever feel normal again?

In the aftermath of a terrorist attack, children, like adults, are on an emotional rollercoaster. Some moments everything feels fine and back to normal; other moments you feel depressed and lethargic. The fact that everyone in the country is going through similar feelings doesn't make it that much better. Explain to your child that it will be like this for a while. Tell her that you, too, feel these emotional swings. Eventually, everything will feel normal again.

Don't expect your child to snap back to normal quickly. Be patient. There's a lot of processing that needs to happen to assimilate the reality of such an event.

Be prepared to listen to your child talk—or play—this through again, and again, and yet again. Much as they are frightened, children may want to reenact the incident constantly, as a way of bracing themselves emotionally for a possible return of the situation. Let them.

In the meantime, do something. Go jogging together, slap finger paint around, play a game with a lot of shouting. Try to discharge some of the excess energy.

Writing, Drawing, and Playing
as Therapy

Writing, drawing, and playing can all aid children in working through some of the angst of trauma. Children often engage in these activities as a way of working through distress or other emotions that they have encountered in everyday life. A child whose mother has yelled at her because she threw cereal all over the floor might scold her doll in a similar manner, as a way of relieving her bad feelings about the scolding.

Following a terrorism situation, as with any trauma, children's enactments of the situation may seem almost too detailed and intense. The very repetition is healing to the child who would otherwise consciously repress the memories of the scary event.

Children may want you to be involved in their play, as occasionally it is too frightening for them to reenact the trauma without you close by. Or they may want the freedom to emote without fear of censure or judgment that playing in privacy affords. Either way, respect their playing, and encourage it.

If the play seems monotonously similar, rather than free-spirited and versatile, it may be the post-traumatic play of a child obsessed with an incident. If the obsessive play incorporates a behavior that is different from your child's normal behavior, seek professional help for your child.

Finally, consider encouraging your child to play, write, or draw with other children who were similarly affected by the events. Group situations can be extremely useful in helping children work through some of their anxieties.

Writing

Suggest your child keep a journal of the event, or write a letter to one of the victim's families. Or write poems, or stories, with the following themes:

- Write about your most scary nightmare
- Write how you felt when you first heard the news
- Write how you feel about it now that it's over
- Write what your life is like now
- Write what people have been saying

You can also simply encourage your child to keep a journal or diary without making suggestions. They may find an open-ended writing process particularly helpful.

Drawing

Get out the art supplies. Sit down with your child, and both of you draw. Don't make suggestions, just draw. Let your child lead, and you follow. Don't do anything too directed. If you feel you must say something, try the following:

- Draw what you feel like right now
- Paint the color you feel
- Draw your life

Or draw or paint squiggles on a piece of paper and let your child turn them into pictures. Then ask them questions about their pictures, and see what they say. Remember, the goal in play therapy is to be as non-directive as possible; you can't regulate the conversation.

Playing

Use puppets or dolls with your child. Or use dress-up clothing.

Again, remember that the goal is not to direct the play so as to "discuss" the events; the goal is to let your child play and see if she is working through the events.

Join in her play and see what she is focusing on. Although you shouldn't direct the play, you can try offering solutions or alternative endings to her play.

Children's play can be as unsettling for the adults around them as children's anger. You may feel uncomfortable watching your child play, either because of the intensity of the play or because of the content. Try not to judge, and try not to let your child see your discomfort.

For Further Reading

There are hundreds of books for adults on how children grieve and experience trauma. The most accessible of the trauma books is Lenore Terr's *Too Scared to Cry: How Trauma Affects Children – and Ultimately Us All.*

Two good adult books on how children grieve are these:
Explaining Death to Children by Earl Grollman
On Death and Dying by Elisabeth Kübler-Ross

A good book for adults on dealing with life's difficult questions is:

When Bad Things Happen to Good People by Harold Kushner

Unfortunately, there are very few books on trauma, war, and terrorism for children. There are many good books on grieving, however, which are worthwhile; here is just a smattering of what is available.

Books for 3-8 year olds:
When Dinosaurs Die by Laurie and Marc Brown
The Dead Bird by Margaret Brown
Nana Upstairs and Nana Downstairs by Tomie dePaoloa
Lifetimes by Bryan Mellonie and Robert Ingpen

Books for 8-12 year olds:
Little Women by Louisa May Alcott
The Big Wave by Pearl Buck
Meet the Austins by Madeleine L'Engle

Books for Teenagers:
A Death in the Family by James Agee
Green Memories by Lewis Mumford
Love Story by Erich Segal